DAD'S TWEED COAT

DAD'S TWEED COAT

Small Wisdoms, Hidden Comforts, Unexpected Joys

by Jim Reed

PREMIUM PRESS AMERICA

Nashville, Tennessee

ISBN 1-887654-13-5

Library of Congress Catalog Card Number 96-69013

Premium Press America books are available at special dis-
counts for premiums, sales promotions, fund-raising, or edu-
cational use. For details contact the Publisher at P.O. Box
159015, Nashville, Tenn. 37215, or phone (800) 891-7323.

1 2 3 4 5 6 7 8 9 10
First Edition

To those who, without even knowing me, taught me to write gently: Ray Bradbury, James Thurber, Walt Kelly, Bob Elliott, and Ray Goulding, all shared the same secret: People are tougher than they appear, and far more frail than they act. Also dedicated to two teachers whose belief in me was unconditional: Helen Hisey and Sadie Logan.

TABLE OF CONTENTS

FOREWORD

IF YOU LIVE IN MY PART OF THE SOUTH AND LOVE BOOKS, sooner or later you are going to meet Jim Reed. Jim has the most interesting old bookstore I've ever seen, but to call Jim's store an "old bookstore" is a bit like saying the ceiling of the Sistine Chapel has a good paint job. In addition to every conceivable kind of old book—Karl Marx rubbing elbows with the Marx Brothers—Jim has a fascinating collection of American memorabilia. Tucked in here and there are circus posters, pinup calendars, three-dimensional movie stand-ups, a seven-foot Santa Claus, a six-foot Sinclair Oil sign, and a complete rural post office from his grandfather's general store in Peterson, Alabama. There are ocean liner menus, mannequins, autographed copies of famous novels . . . oh, my goodness! Where to start looking and, what's worse, where to stop! The Dickens title *The Old Curiosity Shop* comes to mind, but Jim refers to his store as his Museum of Fond Memories. He has a knack for finding meaning in the past and he surrounds himself with books—and things—that bring this meaning into his life.

One afternoon I was in Reed Books trying to figure out how I was ever going to make myself leave, when Jim and I got into a conversation. He knew I was a writer and confided in me that he had a manuscript. He seemed to think I wouldn't be interested, but I was. I wondered what kind of writing would flow from a man who had crafted such an amazing bookshop. I asked him if I could read his work, and he agreed. I had no idea what a treat was in store for me.

Jim's manuscript was a collections of pieces he had written on his daily life. He had been writing these pieces for years, including them in mailings to his best customers who were book lovers and literary folks. Jim's customers liked the pieces, read them to their friends, and wrote letters of appreciation. Jim already had a small, but select, group of people who admired his writing. When I dipped into the manuscript, I found out why. I found something very special.

Jim's writing flows in the tradition of some of the best Southern writers. His gentle, but funny, personality shines through every page. Best of all, Jim has a fresh and unusual way of perceiving the world. He can find comfort, joy, and meaning in the smallest aspects of everyday life. As I read, he led me to one "Ah, ha" after another. I laughed, shed a tear and shook my head in wonder at the things he could make me see. When I finished, I felt uplifted, comforted, and enriched by a new sense of how to see the meaning of life. I sent the manuscript to one of my publishers, George Schnitzer. George and I both feel privileged to play a part in making it possible for others to share the delight of reading . . . *Dad's Tweed Coat*

—Allen Johnson, Jr.

PREFACE

ANYBODY CAN LIVE A LIFE. All you have to do is allow the reflexes to take their course, try not to stop the heartbeat, avoid stopping up all the openings through which you breathe, stay out of the way of oncoming traffic, and avoid dancing with wolves.

What's really hard is to pause and actually take notice of a life.

There have been long periods of my life when I attempted to keep from noticing things, but things always screamed silently at me and made themselves heard anyhow. I gave in and began to record those things that nobody else would bother to record because those things were part of my life, not anybody else's.

And in the process of timidly sharing some of my writings with others, I found that they recognized what I was writing about. Amazing!

They, too, had noticed life but had not bothered writing it down.

So, I'm writing all this down for those who, for whatever reason, don't write it down themselves. Pretend this is your diary, your journey, your journal.

In the process of reading my life, you just may decide to start keeping notes about your own life. Let me know if you do. It'll give me an undeserved jolt of good cheer.

And now, my life: *It was a dark and stormy night . . . .*

Always keep a slight smile on your face. It'll make your enemies think you know something they don't.

—Unknown

Wearing Your Memories

IT'S JUST A TWEED JACKET that's old before its time, but I hate to let it go. I've been wearing it and wearing it and wearing it, and it feels as good as my skin. By now it's about as baggy as my skin, and besides, who needs a new tweed jacket when you've got one that feels this nice? I usually wear it all during the cooler months, most of the time with jeans and tennis shoes or khaki pants and tennis shoes.

Sometimes I vary my wardrobe and wear something besides a black shirt—my usual apparel. Get the shirts at a priest boutique—one of those little stores selling religious stuff. I like 'em because they don't have buttons showing and because nobody else (but priests) wears them.

DAD'S TWEED COAT

So, you'll usually find me going to the post office and the drugstore and the office on a workday (everyday) wearing that old baggy tweed coat, the black or grey priest shirt, and those dirty old tennis shoes complete with clean underwear and an old leather belt and jeans or trousers of some kind. The closest I ever come to dressing up is to dredge out my previous-life dark suit, my current-life red bow tie and one of those priest shirts, along with the standard black shoes and socks that once were mired deeply in corporate intrigue, corporate sin.

The tweed jacket belonged to my father. Since he died, I've taken him with me via the old jacket to such places as relatives' homes; Washington, DC; Radford, Virginia; Cuba, Alabama; Lookout Mountain, Tennessee; Atlanta, Georgia; and home every day, to have him comfortably near the family as we go about our funny and furious business of living.

The old tweed jacket was nice and new-looking when I first put it on soon after the funeral, and I'll have to retire it to the closet after a time, since Daddy wouldn't have liked thinking his clothes ever looked shabby in public. The good memories of my father I can wear all the time, anyhow, so I'd best be about the business of weaning myself and remembering the times before I donned this nice old piece of cloth.

The important stuff my father left me isn't shabby at all

—Jim Reed

LITTLE BIG OLD LADY

YOU WOULDN'T KNOW IT JUST TO LOOK AT HER, but she's a woman who was perhaps typical of America's lower-middle-class housewives of the 1940s and 1950s—before instant everything, before fast food, before automatic, before pre-fab and drive-through and microwave and ready-to-serve.

She's a woman who had to make do with what was already at hand. She came up with three hot meals a day for five kids, and everything was made from scratch.

The margarine had to be yellowed by massaging red dye into it through a cellophane bag.

The cornbread had to be cooked without self-rising or enriched flour, the kitchen heat of the afternoon had to be borne without air conditioning, the oven had to go full blast in the tiny airless bungalow in order to cook anything, the grits and the oatmeal and the cream of wheat and the cakes and the pies had to be cooked from scratch without the aid of pre-packaged ingredients, the diapers had to be washed and re-used and washed and re-used, the clothes had to be sorted and stirred in the bathtub and rinsed and wrung by hand and carefully pinned to a clothesline outdoors unless of course it rained and then she had to go and get everything off the line and turn the house into a magic hanging garden of linens and cottons and nylons until the sun came out and then she had to take them all back outside and hang them up again and then bring them in and sort them and fold them and put them away before the days of anti-static-cling, and then ironing had to be done in the humid and hot summer afternoon by hand while radio soap operas distracted her weariness, and kids had to stay in their domain—the back yard and the front yard—so that she could accomplish all this without aid of dishwasher or maid or power-driven lawn mower.

Back then, she kept kids occupied by feeding them

Kool-Aid and Pepsi-Cola and buying them Collier's Encyclopedia and Junior Classics and Childcraft and comic books and Whitman books and Little Golden Books and Wonder Books.

And bills had to be paid in person by taking the bus with kids in tow, and going to the water works and the power company and the gas company and the mortgage company and then to Woolworth and Kress for treats.

She never had time to be ill or depressed because there was always the next immediate deadline to meet and then her husband would be coming home from work and things had to be on schedule because if they got behind schedule there was no delegating the leftover work to anyone else.

She and her husband worked hard and intensely and never stopped even once to say, "Gee, I'm feeling depressed today—think I'll call in sick," or "Gosh—this just isn't me. I think I'll drop out and do something more fulfilling," or "Why don't we just go on welfare and give up all this pain?"

There simply were no options like that in their generation.

They just kept on keeping on, and their kids all grew up finally and got lives and they had a bit of time together to enjoy retirement before he died, and now here she is, still surviving, still dealing with her grown kids and grandkids and great-grandkids and never letting a day go by without displaying her indefatigable bravery in the line of fire.

Even though she got run over by an automobile a while back and even though she's once again walking when some medical professionals doubted she ever would again and even though she's in her eighties, she hasn't stopped her forward progress and her concern for her family and her willingness to go party with anybody who will go party with her any time of the day or night.

What a woman. Happy Mother's Day every day, Mother. Keep on keeping on, you hear

—Jim Reed

RELATIVE RELATIVITY

DEAR DIARY: EINSTEIN WAS RIGHT. Everything is relative. What Einstein failed to go on to say is relativity is everything. In fact, relativity is everybody.

We are all related in some manner, a fact at once beguiling and frustrating, at times horrifying to think (did I really come from the same evolutionary roots as Saddam Hussein and Princess Di?), and at times provocative (I may share wellsprings with Einstein himself, or Raquel Welch, or even Pee Wee Herman).

If we are all kin, most of us don't like to admit it except when it's convenient. Sometimes, the same folks who go on and on about how they've traced their roots all the way back to King Henry V or the Vikings, are the same folks who don't like to talk about the fact that if they go far enough back before that, they are also kin to Nelson Mandela, Adolf Hitler, Moses, Rube Goldberg, Henny Youngman, and Mother Teresa.

We share a common ancestry—and you have to believe that, whether you're an evolutionist or a religionist.

So, if we're all in the same family, why do we treat cousins and sisters and offspring different from neighbors, foreigners, and aliens? Why is our own blood so much more palatable than a stranger's? Why are my lawn weeds nicer than your lawn weeds?

It's not only a small world, it's a world interwoven with genes and bloodlines and ancestries.

Unfortunately, it's also a world of many fences and few gates, a world of defensive weaponry that can become offensive at any given moment, a world of more "should have's" than "can do's," a world where the meek, though blessed, are often oppressed simply because they do not place aggression at the tops of their priority lists.

Where is the good in the world, then? you ask.

Well, it's like everything else in the universe—the good is there, you simply have to fade the bad stuff out for a while so you can notice it.

An audience laughing at the same humor is sharing a commonality that transcends the petty differences of the moment.

An old man stopping to pat a small child on the head is making a quantum leap in time and, without knowing it, is by the same act massaging the cosmos with a bit of kindness.

A police officer who suddenly and without thinking risks life and limb to save the life of someone who in normal situations wouldn't seem worth the extension of a cordial greeting . . . that officer is unconsciously affirming the fragile but extensive thread of hope that cobwebs the world and makes itself available at the strangest times.

It's out there. You have to either take time to notice it, or act quickly when the kindness urge strikes, so that you won't have time to figure out why you shouldn't be doing something so wimpy as generating an unconditional act of sweetness

—Jim Reed

Twenty-First Century Universal Collecting Procedure

IN THE VERY BEGINNING OF CHILDHOOD there were things you could touch and fondle and smell and rub and truly enjoy, such as . . . coins! You could pick up a coin given you by a kind uncle and feel the ridges around the edge, smell the slightly acrid-metallic odor, and wonder at the figure and words thereon, at the difference between front and back, heads and tails, and wonder who came up with what was supposed to be "head" and what was supposed to be "tail."

Then, if another uncle gave you another silver dollar and another, you could say you were collecting silver dollars. You could hide them safely away in your Littlest Angel cigar box under the bed and meditate on them late at night or during quiet boring afternoon-heated hours and then you could put them all in your pocket and walk around with one hand in your pocket, reveling in the sensuousness of those round, hard, and now warm objects in your small palm, so big and so heavy for their size.

You could spend so much time playing with them that for the rest of your life you would have a physical reaction each time you saw a large coin.

Eventually, the coins would begin to show wear from all the attention, and the metal would take on a different, softer, more friendly glow.

You grow up a few years, hit adolescence and forget about your coins, till one day you see some beautiful glowing coin in an ad or at a flea market and decide that you want to start a collection of your own now that you no longer depend on the kindnesses of uncles long passed.

That's when the startling truth about Twenty-first Century Universal Collecting Procedure hits you in the face.

When you hang around other collectors, you learn that the very worst thing you can possible do is actually touch the coin.

Monetary value is talked about rather than nostalgic rushes of blood to the face.

Resale and investment opportunities intrude themselves from the mouths of experts in the field, and you feel suddenly not so hip in admitting that you just want some coins to touch and play around with.

And so it goes with book collecting.

I used to believe that my most valuable books were the ones I'd read the most, turned down the most pages in, cracked the spine to the best passages in, read till the covers came loose, made notes in.

But when I met other professionals in the field I realized that the coin craze had hit them, too. They turned their noses up at the sight of well-read books, talked of mint condition books and first edition printings and protected dust jackets, and I bought into that in order to get started in book collecting.

But I still sneak off to the corner of my loft and pull the old, worn personal copies out once in a while, the ones I won't sell to anyone else, and feel that old familiar handful of words that I have had intimate contact with for oh so long.

And I am still partial to customers who actually read books and smile inwardly when they touch them.

I have trouble not feeling sorry for those who buy books to see and show but not to escape into and fall in love with

—Jim Reed

LOOKING AHEAD TO THE PAST

ONCE I REALIZED THAT TIME TRAVEL WAS POSSIBLE life has become so much more pleasurable. You see, as time whizzes past and plays tacky tricks on you, life can seem harder, and your feet try each month to sink deeper into molasses, making everything just a bit more difficult and a trifle more achy. As the weight of each day piles itself gleefully upon the day prior and looks forward to the density of the next day and the next, the old shoulders ache and the neck cricks and the bones creak more audibly as you try to swim through this muck.

It won't get any better if you think about it, you know.

So, what's a human to do?

Time-travel!

DAD'S TWEED COAT

There's always a more pleasurable time at the fingertip, ready to spring into wistful life and give you a little charge. What's a smile worth? What's the value of an inward grin? If you gotta go, wouldn't you prefer to wear a mysterious smirk to perplex the undertaker?

There were good times during your life, believe it or not. They didn't occur just to lie fallow and fade to black. They occurred so you could dredge them up for a drug-free jolt to the nervous system when things seem glum, when life seems a bummer.

What was your pleasure? Where was it? When was it? How did it feel, taste, sound?

Was it simple—lying on your back in the back yard, looking at clouds and trying to make animated scenes from them?

Was it complicated—acing an exam you really never thought you'd live through?

Was it secret—something you saw that gave you great pleasure, your little secret between yourself and yourself?

Was it a guilty pleasure—was it a pleasure you must share with an old friend someday, or was it something you've never really done but always enjoy thinking about doing?

Whatever. Time travel doesn't have to be complicated, you know. You can just think about what a carnival smells like, what a meadow feels like barefoot, what a chrome trim looks like in the bright sun, what the first-ever kiss felt like from the first-ever love of your life, what the kiss of your mother felt like when you were just three and beginning to shuck off innocence.

Use your time machine. The experiences are more than you can possibly call up in a lifetime. They are there to replay, freeze-frame, fast-forward, slo-mo, and cherish. And to heck with all those bad times. They aren't worth the effort—unless there was something nice to remember or re-think in the midst of all that grimness

—*Jim Reed*

Want to know how to make God laugh?
Tell him your plans.

—Robert Altman

SEREN-DAMN-DIPITY

As I WAS STRUGGLING, swimming, wading through the hundred-degree-and-all-the-humidity-you-can-eat morning, I remembered that this was the hour that eighty-three-year-old Aunt Margaret would be undergoing cataract surgery, some 500 miles south of here.

Getting into the steaming car to go to work, I felt that pang of regret that comes from knowing finances just can't support desires these days—at least all desires. A few hundred bucks extra would have allowed us to go down and be with her during a time perhaps more trying for us than for her, since she's braver about the painful passages of life than we younger squirts are.

But, you can't do everything—at least in person.

DAD'S TWEED COAT

As the car began climbing the hill on our block, I absent-mindedly looked to the right and saw a nicely dressed and coifed woman in her eighties walking very slowly down the hill, looking right and left in obvious confusion. I slowed down but drove on, wondering what was wrong with this picture.

I suddenly realized that this particular grey-haired denizen was a stranger to the neighborhood, and that her pace, seen through the rearview mirror, was slowing. This was one hot and humid day for someone to be lost.

And, sure enough, she was lost.

I U-turned, drove beside her, and gently asked if I could help. Turned out she had been let off at a bus stop some four blocks back instead of at her destination, had wandered in the direction she supposed to be correct, and was now, I tried pointing out to her, completely lost.

She was perspiring heavily and was walking away from the direction in which she needed to be headed in a declining neighborhood of a city ranked high in the nation in annual homicides. I figured she would pass out later from the heat before coming to anything cool and dry like a drugstore or convenience market.

And she couldn't see very well, to boot, I learned: she was on her way to the ophthalmologist for examination, her eighty-year-old eyes about ready for adjustment, just as Aunt Margaret's.

I put her in the car and took her to the doctor. She politely offered to pay me for my trouble, and I didn't accept. I made her promise to take a taxi home and not to try this wandering about trick again.

She again offered to pay me, but I couldn't tell her the truth—that her name was Aunt Margaret and that I had just now held out my 500-mile-long arm and clasped another person's hand who at that moment was receiving new and better vision, and that somehow everything for a brief intense moment seemed connected to everything else in the universe

—Jim Reed

Going Going

WELL, THERE SHE GOES! One twenty-two-year-old daughter, who has put up with her old man most of her life, is at last going to leap from the nest and try flapping around a bit to see if it's true that the very young can defy gravity simply by sheer will power and hope and exuberance and energy and beauty.

All those years I was merely her daddy she managed to survive all kinds of hazards of life without my help at all. She came through summer camp and the horrors of YMCA after-school camp and many years of dancing the

Nutcracker and months of hauling a cast around and years of braces and the terrors of the first brassiere and the first boyfriend and the first fall-flat-on-the-face while hanging from a monkey bar and head to the emergency room and the first bad hangover and the first see-what-we-can-get-away-with adventures with friends in the late of night and the first job and the first day of college and the dance performances on the road and the first trip to New York City and the first recital of her complete math tables and the first automobile and the first automobile accident and the first apartment and the first college final and the first coming back home to see if the old man has grown up yet.

She got through all these things without my help, and yet she still seems to need me now and then and she still comes to see me and she still calls me and she still remembers to giggle at all my worn-out jokes and she still makes me feel so damned warm inside and she still likes to eat junk food with me and watch bad videos with me and roll her eyes around family members and relatives at the same time I do.

Now what more could I possibly ask for than a

daughter such as this?

And here she is graduating without my help.

And there she goes leading her own life now.

And do you suppose that at some point she will suddenly forget about her old man and have a complete life of her own?

And are these things mutually exclusive?

Her old man will just have to wait and see

—*Jim Reed*

WIND WENDS WAY, WRITING-WISE

LISTENING TO AN ANNOUNCER ON THE LOCAL PUBLIC RADIO STATION talk about the Hubble telescope "winding its way into space" (it's "wending," I tell you, "wending!"), or the local commercial-TV announcer describing neighbors "getting their dandruff up over local crime rates," (I guess getting your dander up can cause stress that can lead to dandruff), or reading in the local fish-shroud that "he lead the group in song," (I suppose if you led the group in song you'd at least get the lead out of their throats), I am tempted to make up my own words, too—after all, making up phrases and words sure beats having to look them up all the time.

Wasn't it William Saroyan who advised writers never

to use a word that they would have to look up first—for fear, I suppose, that the author would not really own the word if it had to be forced through research, thesaurused to death.

I must confess that I take Saroyan seriously on this matter. If I have to look a word up while I'm writing, I know it's not the right word, so I use one that I understand and already own. Later, after the piece is completed, I will look up the word I wondered about, meditate upon it, and perhaps it will crop up in later writings—if, and only if, it flows out naturally.

Of course, this technique doesn't always make for accessible-to-the-reader reading, but it does make for satisfactory-to-the-writer writing.

For instance, last week I realized that the word "stygian" had crept suddenly and independently into two pieces I had written. In each case, it had emerged naturally, and it was the only week in my life that I have used that word. I may never use it again. But it meant a lot to me, and it felt just right in each instance.

I recall that the crossing to Hades is the river Styx. As a youngster, I used to gaze at a Doré etching of Charon, the solitary ferryman who takes those of us who are going Hadesward across.

I never wondered till now why we'll have to get on a ferry to get to Hades. If you're already condemned to go there, are you very worried about drowning if you try to swim across?

Where was I?

Well, anyhow, the word "stygian" seemed to drop right into my puce prose, to describe a situation. In a poem I wrote, "stygian" came up again, but only because it seemed to provide a tactile contrast to the warmth and mystery of interpersonal life that the universe sometimes surprises us with. It was right for the moment.

Whether it was right for the reader in both cases remains for scholars eons from now to decide when this message-in-a-bottle is found and sniffed and probed

—Jim Reed

Basket Case For A Gentleman

THE FIRST TIME I SAW THE BASKET LADY she thanked me for opening the door for her at the post office . . . using a loud and husky voice, "Why, thank you . . . a real gentleman!" Her musical delivery made my morning a little nicer. That, of course, is because I'm of the generation that was often told that being a gentleman was a virtue . . . and, furthermore, virtue was a nice thing to possess.

The basket lady is probably in her late sixties or early seventies. She is dressed, as we would say down here, for Sunday school and her outfit includes makeup, hose and a pleasant smile under her carefully arranged blonde hairdo. She walks slowly, pulling behind her a metal wheeled basket—the kind assistants use to pick up the morning corporate mail.

I see her often, the basket lady, sometimes moving slowly along Fourteenth Avenue South, chatting merrily with herself. Once I went into F. W. Woolworth and saw her eating breakfast at the counter, a bit of grits on her chin and a napkin poised while she smiled across the counter at a sullen waitress. There were other elderly diners at the counter, people who seemed never to have left Woolworth's, people who eat there just to recapture an old memory of what it was like so many moons ago when Woolworth's was a thriving social center in each community, competing with S. H. Kress for the place of honor as bus stop and gathering place for everybody you knew who wanted a dime bag of popcorn that could last an hour. That was back when waitresses were polite even if you didn't tip much, back when you could feel safe leaving your purse and bags on that little ledge beneath the lunch counter while shopping around for one more item in the store.

The basket lady is the only person who has called me a gentleman in decades, and I liked it. Even though it's

sexist nowadays, I still hold the door open for women—
as well as men, if I get there first—and I still smile and
nod to people on the street in tribute to my father and his
generation, who always tipped their ever-present hats to
ladies and gestured to strangers on the street. Perhaps
the memory of those gentler days is why the basket lady
never forgets to smile at passers-by. After all, she's a lady

—Jim Reed

Brother Bryan In The Park

The small park reflected the sun back at itself in the bright and humid afternoon.

A small grey- and black-spotted breast belonged to the proud bird boasting shrilly of birdlike affairs.

A young father sat in the children's swings and methodically pendulumed himself thirty years backwards, using the same motions as his small son in the seat beside him. They both stared contentedly forward, each melting inwardly their unexpressed thoughts—the one looking only at Now, the other thinking how nice Then was.

Another man sat lotuslike on a metal bench and re-

read a twice-unfolded letter, then lay down and stared at the tree-top-crossed skies.

A young couple walked hand-in-hand with a long-stemmed rose and shared unheard secrets.

A pale and disheveled man pored over textbooks and rubbed his temple.

A homeless man sat and absorbed sunbeams, and a young well-designer-clothed man came and sat beside him in a parallel universe.

It was Mother's Day at Brother Bryan Park.

Suddenly, my relatives began materializing where I alone had reigned over this placid and electric Sunday afternoon. My son-in-law came and talked work and problems and movies and kids with me. The mother of my grandchild showed up in new sundress finery and ran after her offspring with a cloned gait, five years old one moment, twenty-five the next. My grown daughters appeared and played and ate and held crucifix-free communion with one another. My son showed up in Army Reserve camouflage and blended himself into our happy gathering, watching his daughter and her mother, then joining them in featherlight softball, while my wife, in a sundress hat, teleported herself into our midst and made things happen between us all, caused the loveliness and the lovingness of the so-sweet evening to become part of another memory no scrapbook could ever re-play with quite the same feelings.

You just had to be there, you know.

Wish you had been

—Jim Reed

I've always thought respectable people scoundrels, and I look anxiously at my face every morning for signs of my becoming a scoundrel.

—Bertrand Russell

THE WRITE RIGHT RITE

I THINK THAT'S WHY PEOPLE WRITE DIARIES, you know . . .
it's easy to get away with outrageous thoughts and
prurient lambastes and scatological diatribes and just
plain foolish confessions, when you're dead. About time
somebody said something about the advantages of being
dead, even though one of my muse mentors, Walt Kelly,
said, "There is no future in bein' dead." Turned out he
was a liar, of course, since the memory of Pogo and other
of his creations seems even stronger now, these many
years after his demise. Anyhow, diaries are great fun to
keep, because you can tell everybody off and never be
around to hear the resultant furor. Another on a long list
of guilty pleasures! Just make sure that somebody even-

tually sees what you wrote, or some of the fun will be missing. Donate said diary to a local archives department and hope that, long forgotten, it will someday turn up in the hands of a bored graduate student who'll get involved in reading it and think how quaint our customs were way back in the 1990s, will think patronizingly how smart we were even back then, and will praise our memorial wordage as being ahead of its time, even as we now praise folks like Montaigne, who, after all, was just writing down stuff that we, too, know about and ponder on each day—such as, the advantages of life, the advantages of death, and the advantages and disadvantages of not being able some days to tell the difference

—*Jim Reed*

TELEPORTATION

LAST NIGHT, HURTLING ALABAMAWARD from Atlanta on the cool passionless multi-laned and impersonal asphalt, I could see star-illuminated frosty clouds drifting high above the carbon monoxide and frantically racing motorists with their boom-boom speakers making windshields vibrate with artificial and unloving sounds. Inside the metal and fiber cocoon of our bullet-shaped vehicle, I drove alone until my wife woke up and reminded me that I am alive and well and married and a part of the world. But before that, while she slept beside me in the careening and Birmingham-aimed space capsule, I was the only person in the universe and the other capsules were meteors barely missing me, making my car shudder. The speed limit went up once the obligatory Georgia Highway Patrol blue-flashed to the side of the highway yet another unsuspecting junker whose occupant could not afford the sophisticated detection devices with which others escaped and laughed their way home. "Racing with the Moon" was a song I heard many times some forty years ago, and I always remember it when I look through the car window and see a planet or star or the orb itself keeping up with me. I remember being told that whoever had written the song had done so after a tragic automobile accident had killed a loved one—one who was racing the moon and became moonstruck and finally lost the lead. The memory always makes me slow down a bit and remain snug in the right lane, smugly sad at all those cars hurtling through the firefly night and never winning the race

—*Jim Reed*

No Flea Markets On Me

I COULD RETIRE IF I COULD ONLY find all the long-lost books my customers need all at once.

I am in the book finding business, and I only find books that nobody else can find. Customers pay me for these, mainly because they want them so badly.

Trouble is, I can't find everything everybody wants in a short period. It takes time to ply my trade, you know.

Would I retire if this happened, if I found every book everybody wants right now?

Or if I won the lottery?

Well . . . no.

I'd worry less about money and spend more time funning myself in the sun.

DAD'S TWEED COAT

What would you do?

Spring fever must be creeping in.

I'd like to go fondle some old books in flea markets and attics and front yards.

I get real excited about some books in particular—such as Armed Service edition paperbacks, leather bound miniature books, Pogo books, women in sundresses on sunny windy days.

Wait—where did that come from?

Must have been something I wrote. It snuck in. Spring, in other words, is here.

The sap is rising . . . and about to get up and go home after he finishes writing this.

Hope your dreams are sweet and bookish, and that you pay fifteen cents at a flea market for a priceless volume you just can't die without

—*Jim Reed*

The Last Grocery Store

FIFTY YEARS AFTER THE GENERAL MERCHANDISE STORE of R. L. McGee in Peterson, Alabama, had become the trade and social center of that tiny coal-mining town, I stood atop a wobbly ladder held sturdy by my uncle Adron and brother Tim and, my balding head reflecting the post-storm sunshine of an Alabama winter day, began the task of removing the "R. L. McGee Gen Merchandise" sign from the front of the now decaying and emptying building.

That was just yesterday, and the sign is now resting in our living room waiting to be installed here in my loft, where I can gaze at it daily and remember the won-derful free-ice-cream-and-candy times I spent in my grandfather's store, a place of wonder for small boys who could run among the shoe soles and needles, axe handles and men's flannel shirts, pork and beans and feed bags, and uncles and cousins and aunts and parents and grandparents who loved to visit there.

Outside, the old dinosaur-emblazoned "Sinclair" signs had long been sucked up by a plastic and too too shiny "Arco" sign, but until recently, gas had still been pumped and kerosene doled out and carbide sold by my late uncle Brandon, whose cigarette always dangled haphazardly over the pump handle, dropping ashes into the gasoline vapors and always somehow managing to just barely avoid explosive chaos.

Inside the store, which was welded to the home of my grandfather and grandmother and uncle Brandon, only echoes and scurrying pests and barely-hidden ghosts wander the concrete and wood floors, and there's little left of the store, the one building that once contained: (1) the town post office, (2) the town Greyhound bus stop, (3) the town movie theatre, (4) the town justice of the peace (Granddaddy), (5) the town Eastern Star star (Grandma Effie), (6) the town humorist (Uncle Brandon),

(7) the town pre-charge-card control center (Granddaddy ran charge accounts on everybody, middle class and poor, black and white alike), (8) the town egg farm, (9) the town marriage center, (10) the town have-Granddaddy-make-your-last-will-and-testament center, (11) the town pre-Disney World circus for kids, where you could always bring in a deposit bottle and get an Orange Crush or a Buffalo Rock or a Grapico or an RC Cola on a hot and barefoot day.

The little rickety store was a Mecca for us kids, and now what we have to show for it is in our hearts and our heads, for, with the removal of the signs, the stripping of the medals and buttons, we will someday soon have only a few artifacts and a bunch of wonderful memories to share of a store and a day and an era and a generation now gone and a hundred years from now completely forgotten

—Jim Reed

A Situation Of Gravity

So if skin is nothing but a body bag, why does everybody I know worry and fret about it all the time?

If skin is merely something to hold your parts together till everything wears out, why is so much importance placed on its every ache and pain and blemish and blush?

What is it about skin that causes otherwise balanced people to scurry through the check-out line with a copy of *Reader's Digest* that gives you ten ways to determine whether you "need" a face-lift or body tuck or nipple pump-up job or whatever they're called?

Why do we strive through youth and raging hormones to become adult, then spend the rest of our lives trying to cover up, obliterate, re-form or corset away the bulges and sags and discolorations we worked so hard to earn?

Gravity is the great mystery of the universe—it's the one thing all beings can wonder at and ponder over and never really quite explain satisfactorily. Gravity is invisible and it is there and it tugs at everything and eventually wins.

Gravity is every place you are, and it is a constant reminder of your mortality and the eventual mortality of everything, including the mortality of mortality.

And gravity, a totally impartial essence, is what makes you have those bags and droops and squashed arches and dangles.

Gravity seasons you and gives your face character, your body a lived-in look, and your grandkids something to laugh at as you struggle to tuck it into garments smaller than—and certainly shaped differently than—your stewed-prune exterior.

This face is quite a mess, but it's my face, and I want to enjoy having it just the way gravity—i.e., God—intends it.

Dad's Tweed Coat

Yes, gravity is God. It is everywhere and in-between everything and totally inaccessible but touching all. Isn't that what we've been taught God is? Trouble is, nobody will buy the concept because gravity can't be controlled, and most folks who make their living off God-ology have a vested interest in keeping God all to themselves and away from the rest of us.

Wouldn't it be a hoot if I were right—if God really is gravity, and I discovered it while writing on this very page? And wouldn't it be even more of a hoot if knowing this made not a particle of difference to anyone in the universe but

—Jim Reed

HOTTER THAN . . . HERE!

IT'S HOTTER THAN . . . WELL, HOTTER THAN HOTNESS here in Alabama . . just the thing you westerners and Yankees and Britishers and Canadians would expect me to say this time of year, in August, judging from the stereotypes of the Deep South you may have seen during the past millennium on TV, heard on radio, read in papers and books.

If you've never been down here to visit, you'll have to rely on the missives of yours truly and the reports of others you know who've ventured into our climes and climbed back out sweating and puffing but remembering, too, the sweet smell of honeysuckle growing wild around the hedges, the browned and healthy Southern belles in summer togs, the babies running huskily through a mud puddle after a humid and steamy shower and a harsh-sun-again ten minutes later.

The South is a mixture these summer days of unbearable but sweet heat contrasted spasmodically with freezing temperature air conditioning in stores and theatres and service stations.

Alternating between the frying pan and the freezer section all the time here, some of us wish we'd never experienced air conditioning. It's addictive, but it weakens your chances of surviving in the heat when you trot outdoors to the air-conditioned car.

Pre-air-conditioned Southern heat was so sensual. You couldn't get rid of it, so you succumbed with the knowledge that everybody else was sweating, too; you weren't standing out as much as you felt.

The heat is wonderful if you just let go and stop fighting it.

But, if you've got a job to do and people to work around and family to be nice to, you just have to cool off and dry off now and then so you won't look like Rod Steiger as an unhygienic Southern sheriff or James Whitmore in one of those endless World War II jungle movies.

You feel slimy and grungy, but you can always cool off with a Coke or a shower or a sudden illogical breeze on the front porch.

Quickie salvation, then back to smoldering.

Once you come down here to stay a while, though, you don't want to leave. After all, August only comes once a year, and the rest of the time life is polite and slow and actually stimulating—not nearly so nerve-shattering as traffic clutter and freeways and tourist traps in other parts of the country.

But even true blue Southerners romanticize other parts of the U.S.

New York seems exciting to many, New Orleans seems like party town, Washington, D.C., seems like an attractive Sodom, and the West Coast is supposed to be the New World of youth and fad and culture.

Southerners like traveling to these places, and we fantasize about moving to them when we're there. But something draws us back here, to where our roots have broken off into the soil and are now indistinguishable from the red clay and the hummingbirds and the blue smoke clinging to the hills.

So, we cling with our fingertips and accept the yin and yang and write notes to our friends elsewhere and visit them once in a while and always return with fond memories and vague fears that things won't be the same when we get back here.

But they always are.

They always are

—*Jim Reed*

JIMFOOLERY

IF YOU'RE READING THIS YOU MUST BE HANGING IN THERE despite the fact that we've just survived another April Fool's day.

People live through April Fool's cautiously these days and with less humor, it seems.

Each newscast in its reportage of more and more showbiz and sportsbiz news and its concentration on tit-illating bits about senators and movie stars and rock stars and the love life of celibates and the conniving of rise-from-the-flames evangelists and their former slea-zoid girl- and boyfriends . . . each news report seems in and of itself to be one which should end with the announcer grinning all eighty-seven teeth into the camera and yelling, "April Fool!"

But it doesn't happen.

There are just so many stories that can't really be true (and even if they are shouldn't really be true) that it's difficult to look for a good old-fashioned joke or harmless prank.

So, the only reference to April Fool's day I heard was a radio interview with an expert on the sociological significance of *Gilligan's Island* to twentieth century North American culture.

And it was just as serious as half the other stuff on the same radio show.

Our local paper each day prints long lists of people who have died, but no lists of people who've been born. It prints front-page stories about trucks turned over on the interstate but not one story about a small child who's had a knee-scrape on the playground and went through more new-experience trauma than all the bored motorists combined who had to sit and wait for the truck to be moved so they could get on to better things.

There are reports of somber speeches delivered before the Rotary Club but not one story about a dad who finally got up enough courage to say "I love you" to his teenage kids.

There are entire columns on how much each movie made last week but nothing about the deeply felt tears that came as a result of one homemade movie shown at a family reunion of people long gone away but lovingly remembered.

The really big news is predictable and as packaged as a Big Mac, but the simple unadorned events that keep people getting up in hope each morning are never reported. Maybe it's better that we turn on our memories and play these events in our minds. Don't think we can trust such precious stuff in the hands of the media. Know what I mean

—*Jim Reed*

The Earth Overhead

Above my head in the book loft there floats a foot-wide, thirty-foot-long red orange yellow green kite, waving in the air-conditioning breeze and making me look up occasionally to remember a time far gone, when my small daughter and I stood in the abandoned parking lot of the old Liberty supermarket on Greensprings Highway and held on to the longlong string for dear life, the string that kept the world from breaking loose and floating away from that wonderful solid stationary kite around which the entire universe moved.

The asphalt under our feet felt light as seafoam and the kite weighed a million pounds and we wanted so much to climb that silver strand and reach deep into the rainbow kite and bring up the mystery of being, hold it in our hands for a few precious seconds, then let it fly away from its kitebound center and travel to a place where it could make someone else intensely happy for a few ticks

—Jim Reed

It's not that I'm afraid to die. It's just that I don't want to be there when it happens.

—Woody Allen

Life Before Death?
Let Me Get This Straight . . .

OF COURSE, AN EVEN GREATER FEAR THAN OF DYING is that I will have died never having lived. To the profound and universal question, "Is there life before death?" you can add the equally provocative and certainly more immediate question, "What's for dinner?"

Mainly because you can ask great questions all day or even proffer wonderfully sanguine answers day in and day out, but, as Omar Khayyam kept telling us, no matter what you learn or feel or do, you are basically gonna exit via the same door you used to enter.

So where does that leave us fearmongers and tremblers? Do we spend our time whimpering and wailing, or do we just assume the obvious and deal with it—the obvious being no matter how people present themselves to the world, each lives with the same share of terrors and thrills.

DAD'S TWEED COAT

You can sit contemplating your navel.

You can sit contemplating the navels of others.

You can sit envying or enjoying navels.

You can sit classifying or declassifying navels.

Or you can decide that navels are as important as supernovae, as much a part of the black hole cosmos as love letters and sweet peas, daggers and gin, gondolas and gazebos . . . cuticles and, well, navels.

The great questions laze comfortably upon my dust-soaked bookshelves alongside the frivolous questions. Bertrand Russell squeezes next to Anton LaVey, Vonnegut smirks beside Huxley, Ray Bradbury looks across the room at Tennyson and Whitman, and Joseph Campbell lies dangerously near Anais Nin while D. H. Lawrence thumbs his nose at Thomas Aquinas, even though I suspect that a conference at which these resurrected notables sat eye-to-eye, roundtabled with one another, would be a funny and fantastic sight to behold, an experience to be enjoyed, and a way to learn that they all have in common the entrances and exits which they did not or will not escape

—Jim Reed

OLD BOOKIE GETS OLDER AND POORER

I'M IN THE OLD BOOK BUSINESS. I find old out-of-print books for people, and when things are going really well, people actually pay me for the books I find for them.

You'd think people who deal in old books would be flush—that is, wealthy.

But the only flush I feel is the one that comes when somebody I'm late paying money to calls and reminds me.

People who deal in old books are not rich.

Oh, well, money isn't what this book stuff is all about, anyhow, is it?

For those who answer that money is why they're in the old book business, good luck. I don't know any among us who are rich strictly from the sale of old books. But there's always hope . . . foolish though it may be.

DAD'S TWEED COAT

Bookies are made of dream-stuff, and they are happiest in their fantasies, noses poked like thick bookmarks into tomes that leak secret, quiet pleasures.

I still catch myself reading something exciting in public, and looking up to see if anybody can tell what my mind is going through. As a kid, if there was a naughty passage in a book, I would be afraid someone nearby would know just by looking at my face or hearing the loud rush of blood and neurons in my cranium.

Of course, they couldn't—mainly because my *Mad* was stuck inside *Scientific American* for show—while around my friends, I hid the *Scientific American* inside the *Mad*.

I think about that now and then, when, going through an estate of books, I find a book with its dust jacket turned inside-out—a sure sign somebody was trying to hide something. Mainly because most folks threw away the dust jacket when the book arrived.

Once I found a sex manual done thus—full of harmless and misleading turn-of-the-century information and preachments.

Another time, it was a book on group sex—with no pictures! Another time, the jacket was hiding papers—

minutes of a secret society dedicated to something or other—it's around here somewhere.

But I'm happy to see that some people still read in public—as distasteful or incomprehensible as that may seem to some.

So, when I'm scarfing something fast at a local chain gang restaurant, I get a chuckle out of seeing what a young executive is reading (some detective-adventure series) or what a young waitress on her break may be reading (a Krantz-type glitz and hype book . . . what my daughter calls a "slut book." What the heck—it's a book, and it shows the holder probably can read).

I started out on what most folks in the fifties considered to be trash—but the trash of science fiction and detective yarns and adventure stories led me into more fertile fields later on, so it was worth it.

It is still nice to read some trash once in a while, 'cause you find out that some of those folks were really good writers simply stuck in a genre to make a living. Sounds vaguely familiar

—Jim Reed

*I'm an idealist: I don't know where I'm going
but I'm on my way.*

—Carl Sandburg

All Right, OK, Life Wins One

Have I got anything to be thankful for right now, and do you have anything to be thankful for right now, and do we always have to wait till the end of the year to wax eloquent about what life is all about and to make resolutions that if kept could cause revolution and perhaps if truly kept would mean an advance in evolution?

Nah.

We don't have to, but it just seems the thing to do anyhow and anyway I can't seem to stop my fingers at the keys and this is the thankfulness they're trying to communicate for the moment:

1. I'm glad I was able to get up this a.m. and struggle through another day.
2. I'm glad my family is OK and my ma and

brothers and sisters are OK and my neighbors are doing all right and my remaining aunts are OK and my uncles are doing well and, well, I'm glad for anybody I love who's doing OK right now, and I hope they'll keep on doing OK here or in another dimension someday, since my hoping they'll be OK forever as I know them on this earth is highly unrealistic.

3. I'm thankful for all the bookies out there who love books and what they mean and how they heal and how they remind us of our commonality.

4. I'm glad for the sweetness of breath and breathing, and here's hoping all smokers will decide to chuck all smoking materials and see what real air is all about.

5. I'm glad that I don't try to instruct—or preach—or proselytize—as often as I get older, since it is meant well but doomed to failure anyhow.

6. And, well, I'm just feeling right good right now and I hope you are, too

—*Jim Reed*

I can't take a well-tanned person seriously.

—*Cleveland Amory*

THE TANNING I DESERVE

WHICH BRINGS TO MIND my need to compose a list of
*Things I Definitely Won't Be Caught Alive Doing This
Summer Or Any Other Summer If I Can Help It:*

1. Buying a short-sleeved knit shirt with a little alli-
   gator or any other kind of animal on it
2. Sucking my gut in at the beach each time a female
   passes (my gut is beyond sucking in, anyhow)
3. Wearing a baseball cap anywhere (your IQ is
   automatically reduced by twenty points when
   you don one of these things, and I need all the
   IQ I can muster)
4. Wasting away again in Marguerita-Land
5. Joining a country club
6. Joining anything
7. Stopping at every Stuckey's on the highway
   (unless, of course, I'm accompanied by someone

under six years of age)

8. Going to a shopping mall

9. If possible, also, avoid strip malls

Other things I definitely won't be caught doing this summer:

10. Watching *Love Connection, Wheel of Fortune,* Judge Wapner or much of anything else on TV

11. Saying things like, "Far out!" or "I'll get back to you," or "Give me high five," or "Let's do a movie"

12. Taking anything very seriously for more than ten minutes

13. Trying to figure out how to fill in one of those Ed MacMahon mail-outs so that I won't be disqualified from winning $10 million dollars

14. Reading anything called a "blockbuster"

15. Reading lists of things people won't be caught alive doing this summer or any summer

You may well ask how anyone can survive a hot summer without doing some of the above. I'll let you know in the fall

—*Jim Reed*

So little time and so little to do.

—Oscar Levant

FEELING GOOD ALL UNDER

EVERY TUESDAY MORNING, the laundry freshly done and most things in their place, I pick out the newest pair of undershorts in the drawer and slide them on. As the week progresses or regresses, I put on a fresh pair each day (yes, I do take off the used pair before doing so) and try to face the world with strong and white undergirdings bolstering a flagging confidence.

You know what happens next, of course. By the end of the week and through the weekend, I run out of the newest pairs and start digging down into the drawer for older, slightly ragged shorts until, at last, by Monday I am starting the week off with underwear that is holy but not righteous, as my Ma used to say.

The pair I'm wearing now is the most tattered I own, since the laundry is a day late.

Now just suppose that this is all metaphoric, and just suppose that the state of my underwear is roughly equivalent to my state of mind and level of energy?

What would happen if one Tuesday morning I began the week wearing the raggedest underwear and progressively turned to newer pairs as the week waned? Would my attitude be thus affected, would I be saving my high-self-esteem underwear for the most worn-down and wearisome part of the week—thus giving me an extra boost to make it crawling through Saturday night toward the Day of Rest on Sunday?

Maybe, if this works, I will no longer find myself sitting in my ragged underwear on my favorite equally ragged easy-chair on Sunday afternoon, staring into space and dozing, trying to rev up my juices for the week ahead.

The secret of life-energy may be in here somewhere.

I mean, don't we all still believe in magic, and isn't

that why we keep getting up in the morning and trying to tackle each day anew with the idea that there's just got to be something better about this dawn?

Without this magic-potion kind of thinking, we're just another bunch of trembling primitives waiting to be eaten or run over, and taken to the emergency room with—horror of horrors—ragged underwear

—*Jim Reed*

Happening Just Happens

Life just seems to happen to me . . . or is it that I happen to life? Would life even be if I weren't happening to it? And if it is the case that life is happening to me, rather than I to it, does it make one whit of difference (notice how whits always come in ones . . . you never hear about two or even ten whits of difference) in the universal scheme of things?

There, now that I've lost the average reader, this particular note can get down to communicating with the true-blue loyal reader. Probably the only people left reading at this point are

    1. people who will read just about anything out of sheer boredom;

2. people who feel a certain loyalty to the book since they're this deep into it;

3. people who hope that no matter how vague and meandering this page is, the last line or two—the punch line—will save it;

4. people who are just about to doze and don't have the energy to throw the book across the room;

5. my mother, who will apparently read anything I write and feel proud of it (hurrah for moms!);

6. people who keep reading, hoping that I'll make another technical error so they can point it out to me;

7. and people who just like delving into personal works of literature.

Now, where was I?

Oh, yes, about life in the hereafter and the herebefore: Is life happening to me or am I happening to it? Wanna know the answer? And, if so, what good would it do to know the answer? Is it better to just muddle along and be surprised by the next event or thought, or is it better to have all the answers and know all the formulas and have infinite knowledge about everything and everyhappening? Is knowledge necessarily a good thing, or is it better to know very little and guess even less and just roll with the dice of the universe, hoping it'll all come out for the good or at least for the indifferent?

Oops! Another stack of books just fell over in the back of the shop . . . Let me see . . . what book is this that I'm practically stepping on? *Prose Works Other Than Science and Health* by Mary Baker Eddy. Where in the world did that come from? Each day, I find books in my stacks that I didn't know I had. The book falls open to this page, and I read:

> When Aristotle was asked what a person could gain by uttering a falsehood, he replied, "Not to be credited when he shall tell the truth."

Oh, well, I guess I can end this patter now. This quotation is obviously a sign, and I should spend the rest of the week contemplating it. On the other hand, look at it this way: If I have lied to you on this page, you won't credit me when I finally do say something true. On the other hand, does it follow that if I have told the truth on this and many other pages, you could be in danger of not being able to tell when I finally do lie to you?

Either way is dangerous, wouldn't you say?

Good thing Aristotle said that. If I had said it, it would disappear as soon as this small book evaporates into the ozone layer.

Take stock of each precious moment this week, and let the dice-roll itself be the thing . . . and remember that the dots facing down on the dice are as important as the dots facing up

—Jim Reed

JUICE OF THE GODS

HE WAS COMPLETELY OUT OF JUICE.

Completely out of the force that fed his Muse.

Completely out of the running for cosmic insight and understanding.

He sat limp, dumbly staring at the keyboard, hoping that words would come and rise up and take over his fingers and make syllables, then sentences, then paragraphs, then Great American Novels galore.

But nothing happened.

He sat limp, staring morosely at the blank computer screen, feeling the faint radiation seeping into his brain and attacking his enfeebled thoughts and sucking them dry of life.

And nothing happened.

He sat limp, hoping that profundities would stir inside him and dribble over onto the machinery and create beautiful thoughts that would cause little children to clap their hands and old grumpies to chuckle and hide their mouths.

Lots of nothing continued to come forth.

He sat limp, wondering why his mouth was dry, his palms damp, his ears ringing, his mind racing, his thoughts crusty and useless.

With blankness on the screen screaming at him.

He sat limp, admiring those who could always express themselves in ringing tones and glowing words.

And at that moment, he realized that what was going on was his writing, what was going on was what he had to say, what was seeming to be void was exactly the right thing to put down on screen on paper for comrades in writer's block hell to share and find comfort in.

His fingers started to move and move and move

—Jim Reed

Junker Junkie

WELL, SHE'S STRUGGLING to get that big junker of a belch-
ing-fume car into a parallel parking space in front of
Tony's Terrific Hotdogs up on Second Avenue North in
the tattered remains of downtown and the kid beside
her is screaming its head off and she's trying to shut it
up and at the same time keep the lit cigarette from
falling off the hand she's using to guide the big power-
steeringless vehicle into some crooked semblance of a
resting position and it's hot and muggy and steamy
already and it's only 9:30 on a Saturday morning for
God's sake and the car's air conditioning system died
about ten years ago and was never resuscitated and her
bangs are beginning to mat to her forehead and she's

hoping that the drugstore across the street from Tony's is open on Saturdays because she has to get some Preparation H for her invalid mother and her absentee husband is three years behind on the child-support payments and her sleazeball lawyer keeps sending bills to get her to pay for the work he's done to try and get the guy to make his child-support payments and the lawyer sure managed to generate a lot of paperwork that never quite caused the fictitious payments to start appearing in the mailbox but he expects to get his attorney's fees anyhow which means that she is basically supposed to start paying the child support fees she isn't getting from her estranged husband to this attorney so that even if the support money started coming in it wouldn't do her any good because she'd have to turn around and pay them to the lawyer and how did she get herself into this mess in the first place?

Well, she guessed it had all started one adolescent evening at Roebuck park when she decided that intimacy and marriage would have to be better than living with broken parents in a broken home within a broken neighborhood in a broken city so she stopped saying no after the hundredth time and said yes just one time and that about wrapped up her date with fate and determined the course of the next fifty-odd years of her life unless some miracle occurred to change all that and since being a Baptist hadn't seemed to help much about all she could hope for now was a UFO abduction or the lottery or Geraldo or a good horoscope to change her life and she could not imagine what else might change her life except maybe if she stopped worrying about her no-good husband and no-good lawyer and decided to say yes just one time to that good-looking beeraholic neighbor with the relatively new pickup truck who kept asking her out just maybe if she said yes to him he might save her and change her life and help her get this goddamned junker fixed and sweaty screaming kid made happy and her invalid mother the correct kind of medical care and then life would be just about complete, wouldn't it

—*Jim Reed*

THROUGH THE LOOKING GLASS
IF ONLY I COULD SEE IT

I GUESS IT'S BETTER TO SEE THROUGH A GLASS UNFOCUSED THAN TO CURSE THE DARKNESS . . . or something like that.

I have contacts. ("I don't care who you know, lady, you're going to get a ticket.") No, I mean I wear contact lenses.

But you see I only wear contact lenses in order to see things far away. (As Steve Allen once said when asked why he didn't replace his hornrims with contact lenses, "I do wear contact lenses—but that's so that I can find my glasses" or words to that effect.)

If I'm wearing my contact lenses I can see you way over there, but I can't see anything in focus if it's three feet away or nearer. So, when I'm wearing my contacts I have to wear reading glasses, carefully selected from the vast array of designless creations sold at the drugstore.

That means I wear contacts so that I won't have to wear glasses, but I wear reading glasses when I wear contacts so I can read and see other necessary details of life.

When I don't wear contact lenses, I wear other eyeglasses—one expensive prescription pair to see things at a distance and one expensive prescription pair to see things fifteen inches away. In order to see anything closer than fifteen inches, I have to remove whatever glasses I am wearing and get my face about eight inches from an object in order to see it, which is the cheapest way to read—requires no eye doctor or prescription whatsoever.

What I really need is three pairs of glasses when I don't wear contacts—one pair with which to see you way over there, one pair with which to see the evening paper, and one pair with which to see what I am reading up close—such as turn-of-the-century works that defy conventional eyeglasses.

So, let's see: that leaves me with a lot of eyeglasses to

keep up with. But halt—I have more eyeglasses than that. When I am wearing my contact lenses and driving into the sun, I have a pair of drugstore sunglasses that I can put on. When I am driving without my contact lenses but with the glasses for distance vision, I can wear some drugstore clip-on sunglasses when driving into the sun. When I am driving into the sun with neither my contacts nor my distance eyeglasses on, I have to wear a pair of expensive prescription sunglasses to keep from dying too soon.

And, as my mother has said for sixty years, with all this assistance I still can't see very well.

I do miss the clarity of glassless lensless vision. When I was a kid I could see anything anywhere, particularly things nobody thought I could see or, better still, things nobody wanted me to see.

Then, in adolescence, my father had to take me for my first eye examination and my first pair of distance vision eyeglasses. On the way home from the optical shop I looked out of the car window and suddenly realized that lawns were not hazy carpets of green—they actually consisted of individual, clearly distinguishable blades of grass! For a while I was seeing the world for the first time all over again.

In later years, when I saw Buckminster Fuller in person, he reported that he had been practically blind for the first few years of his life but didn't know it and didn't have eyeglasses till he had already learned to experience the world in patterns and designs rather than details. I felt better about my own vision when I heard that, for I don't really know how long I'd been seeing the world through fuzzy Vaselined lenses . . . but I do think that in many ways the world was a bit clearer then than it ever has been since

—Jim Reed

The Bad The Real Bad And The Uglified

So you're standing there in the bathroom not only naked but nude, water dripping from your hairy body, soap stinging your right eye while your left hand gropes for facial tissues and your right hand brings a cotton-tipped stick to your ear, when all of a sudden your wife walks into the steamy-mirrored cubicle so quickly that it's too late to suck in your gut or try to look a bit younger, too late to arrange your hair to carefully cover the bald spot on the back of the head, too late to cloak your birthday garb with sag-camouflage or loosely-fitted clothing to hide the floppy handles, too late to shave and look shiny, too late to fix yourself up so that you can make a reasonably dignified grand entrance into the morning and hope she remembers something of the slim, tight, and spry guy she first laid eyes on so long ago.

Oh, well, this is me, and it is not necessarily a pretty sight. As you get older and the body bag loosens, thins, and droops, you have to look outside your vanity for other ways to feel reasonably presentable, and you hope that, even though the packaging is a bit dated, the intrinsic product will be just as good—in fact, in some ways, you hope that the product will be seen as even better, like an old wine is supposed to be.

I've been marinated by time, and I hope that those around me can find a nice aspect to the process and can savor the knowledge and experience that make for such a vintage marinade. Those who've been conditioned to see only my appearance will judge me to be just another overweight bald guy, and those whose curiosity enables them to look with x-ray vision beneath the leathery facade may be pleasantly surprised to find an interesting and jovial male child inside, just waiting to share good conversation and wonderful ideas and philosophies, or at the very least to share a smile and a word of goodwill

—*Jim Reed*

CLARION IS AS CLARION DOES

A BRILLIANT SUNNY CRYSTAL CLEAR BREATHABLE CLARION DAY TODAY, a day to drive to work and reflect upon the wonders of paradox, a day to make you feel guilty for working but work you must because you know you'll feel guilty not doing it, a day to forget that just recently you were driving along depressed while listening to the squarunch squarunch squarunch of your faulty windshield wipers imperfectly rubbing away rain mixed with aerial scum, a day to remember that life, in all its awesome and frightening variety, can be awful and awe-inspiring at the same moment, that one brief inhalation of beauty, one quick and silent second, can bring unexpected joy in the midst of almost any bad situation.

DAD'S TWEED COAT

If you get just enough of those nice moments of inspiration strung along to separate the cruddy and seemingly insufferable times, you feel you can keep on keeping on, you can continue making one step fit right in front of the previous step, you can take a moment to reflect upon the inner core of you that is still a bright and happy child, pat it on the head and encourage it to stick around yet another day because you know that tomorrow is going to bring lots of stuff that will require comic relief and joyful distraction to break it down into its manageable components

—Jim Reed

GLASS RAINBOW

"POPPY, THERE'S A RAINBOW IN YOUR GLASSES!" The tinny voice of a small five-year-old redheaded urchin focused my wandering mind. I stopped at the door, and looked down over the armchair in the living room at Jessica, who was smiling cheek to cheek.

"What?" I asked.

"There's a rainbow in your glasses!" Jessica repeated. I looked beyond her at the morning cloudless sun beaming in and realized that my Coke-bottle-bottom eyeglasses must have been picking up the sun and tossing its rays into a prismatic wonderland for Jessica's eyes only.

I grinned and beamed her smile back at her, enjoying the moment.

Then, it was out the door and to the car, a toddling lunch-pail carrier at my side, her fist tightly holding a damp quarter for milk.

Some mornings, Jessica can't seem to remember how to strap herself into the seat; other times, she defiantly does it herself and don't you try to help her. This time, just for a test, she claimed she didn't know how and I had to lean over her jelly-mustachioed face to grab the strap and pull it over her lap.

The radio shot war words at my belly, and I decided to turn it off for a while.

"Why'd you do that?" Jessica again.

"What?" Me again.

Jessica: "Why'd you turn off the radio?"

I grunted and listened instead to the sunshine and closely watched the asphalt whooshing under the car. I was humming a song about the sunny side of the street. Jessica looked over me and beyond my shiny pate to the sun that was racing alongside the car, making the east all yellow and white.

"The sun is on the sunny side of the street," she remarked with hand-clapping delight.

So it is, so it is, I grumbled.

How can you maintain an early-morning bad mood when there's so much sunshine coming at you from inside the car, as well as from without?

We maneuvered the cool white vehicle to the front of the school, I punched the button to release Jessica's seat belt, yelled "I love you!" to the red streak, who turned for a second, repeated what I'd just said, and disappeared into the sunshiny morning air. Here's hoping your grumbly morning finds you with a rainbow in your glasses

—Jim Reed

E = A Kind Old Man

THE SEASON IS UPON AND ON TOP OF US, and we automatically search our dusty pasts for perfection and the purity of heart we're almost certain we once had lo those many solar circuits ago. That is, we search till we are presented with a pure and holy moment right before our gauzed eyes, the very place we failed to look.

My friend of ages past, who now lives in Washington, D.C., kept telling me she wanted to take me to see Albert . . . I just had to see Albert, she kept saying while we were visiting her recently.

So, one night in the still and cold darkness on a famous boulevard near the seat of human power in North America, we made our trek to see Albert. There, seated beneath the godly stars, and atop a field of fabricated stars, sat Albert, ruminating upon the universe, a larger-than-life-itself presence who at once seems both dignified and cosmos-struck. The impressionistic and truly wonderful statue of Albert Einstein, star-molder whose thoughts had toyed with the universe and thus begotten users and abusers—those who sought to re-form the world in peace and those who sought to control through fear the very solemn and gentle people like Einstein, who simply want to be left alone to live and eventually, with grace, dissipate into the stars once more.

The statue is a magnificent tribute to the human gossamer spirit that brings us joy and now and then gets us into trouble.

Albert just sits there, gigantic, small, solitary . . . holding a writing pad in his lap with a few simple formulae jotted down, his sandals and sweater and flowing hair the very symbols that bring nonviolent power to a moment in time, the same kind of power expressed by Gandhi's white-robed and sandaled and shiny-pated presence.

DAD'S TWEED COAT

The sculptor had done the right thing, for Albert's statue is not your typical noble-horse-astride general nor your toga'd God nor your brave-in-battle fighter. Albert's statue is made to touch. You can sit on his lap, finger the formula, gaze next to him at the star-scattered universe. He is hidden from direct view, so he's not beckoning tourists.

He is waiting to be discovered in the middle of a cold and quiet night, where he sits and contemplates the uncontemplative and thinks private thoughts—perhaps even the kinds of thoughts we all have the right to think, too

—Jim Reed

ITSY BITSY TEENY WEENY POST-ITS

THOSE LITTLE BITTY PIECES OF PAPER that are always stuffed in my pockets—where do they come from and why can't I remember what they're about half the time?

They not only appear in my pockets, they are floating around my car floor, post-it-ed to my typewriter, stuck inside my calendar, and hiding out under a stack of books and bills.

Frustrating but intriguing, these small and odd-shaped shards of my existence. They seem to leak out of my brain and spill onto napkins, the backs of deposit slips, the tops of receipts and sometimes even on the insides of book jackets. They all seemed important enough to write down at the time, I presume.

Here's one: "Putnam 800 631-8571 MJ Parson MTOPB."

Here's another: "Spires!"

Yet another: "Heavy Western Meat."

Another: "You're just as good today as you were yesterday, only today you can feel it."

Here are some more notes to myself: (1) "The moving blades have power"; (2) "The electric socket"; (3) "Losing Weight: People will wonder if I'm ill"; (4) "Djuna Barnes, Frank Pharcellus Church, Virginia O'Hanlon"; (5) "42 Lower Sloane London 730-5706."

And so on.

Well, just writing them down in this column brings some of their reasons for existence to light.

For instance, "Putnam" has to do with ordering an in-print book through one of those 800 numbers that is eternally busy and thus seldom utilized.

"Spires" refers to the fact that I collect church spires (the tops of old, demolished churches). So far, I've only obtained one, so this may not qualify quite yet as a collection.

Items (1) and (2) must refer to the inherent power of

seemingly harmless objects—guess I was going to write a poem about it.

Item (3) is a meandering thought about maybe just maybe getting around to losing weight one of these days like when I'm ninety-seven years old.

Item (4) is a research list. Do you know who these famous people were?

And item (5) has to do with a friend who will be in England on a certain date while my daughter is dancing there this fall.

"Heavy Western Meat" is a sign I saw in a grocery store window on the east side of town. I had never heard the term.

Wow! That was pretty good. I remembered most of them! This is not usually the case, folks, but thanks for the therapy session. I feel better even if you now feel puzzled

—Jim Reed

UNNECESSARY NECESSITIES

THE THINGS EVERYBODY IS NEVER WITHOUT seem to be the very things there is simply no human need for.

WhattamItalkingabout!?

Well, let's see if I can make a list. *Things Everybody Has With Them Almost All The Time That They Don't Need:*

1. Panty hose. The only people who seem to really need them are convenience store robbers.

2. Pepto-Bismol. Just sit and think calm thoughts a couple of times a day. You'll never again have to be caught walking down the street with pink stains around your lips.

3. Hair spray or other hair stiffeners, straighteners, crookeders, curlers, wavers, bodyers, tinters, bleachers, and replacers and removers. If nobody

used 'em, nobody would think they needed 'em.

4. Deodorants. If everybody smelled like people, nobody would notice it. Of course, it would take a brave person to be the first to quit this habit.

5. Razors, electric and manual. Whatever happened to body hair? We love it thick on top of the head, but we hate it on the face or under the arms or on the legs.

6. Bras. Scratch this one—nobody will believe my motives are pure. And they're not.

7. Skin softeners and tighteners and bleachers and lubricants and cleansers and coverers. If everybody looked like people . . . (see 4, above).

8. Name brands on the outside of clothes. Why be a walking ad and not be paid for it?

9. Lists of *Things Everybody Has With Them Almost All The Time That They Don't Need.*

If you want to add to this, lemme know

—Jim Reed

ROUTINE TRAUMA

HE WAS ALREADY ON AUTOMATIC FOR THE MORNING; he had just left the house and started into motion the machine that would eventually get him to work.

The car drove itself to the post office, then on to the left turn that would head him toward town and book-shop. Without absorbing the sight of the car in front of his, he knew that it had started to cross the same inter-section he would be going through seconds later. The car ahead dead-centered the road at the same moment another downhill racer came from his right and demon-strated that two objects have a lot of trouble occupying the same location at the same time.

He didn't hear the crash till later memory served up

a complete talkie, but he did see the collision clearly, as if the windshield were a motion picture screen and he a popcorned audience of one. The two waltzing cars slammed onto a curb, causing a couple of workmen to jump aside just in time to avoid adding to the statistics. He sat in the car, wondering whether to park or leave his car in the middle of the road.

Something in the well of his soul cringed in advance, readying itself for the possibility of observing blood and suffering and death—things he had not penciled in on his calendar.

He parked and walked over to a mutilated car in which a young woman sat trapped and dazed. The driver of the other car got out and walked around, trying to remember what you do in situations like this. Someone went to call the police but failed to tell them that this was anything more than a fender-bender, which probably explained why it took so very long for anyone in authority to arrive.

Meanwhile, the young woman was panicking, beginning to breathe rapidly and complaining of chest pains. She was strapped to the driver's seat, unable to leave the car because of the crushed door. He put his hand on her warm and damp forehead and spoke to her quietly, remembering how much the simple touch of his father's hand on a very young forehead had healed him instantly so many years ago of fever and pain.

He didn't know what else to do for her.

Other people showed up, spent a lot of time looking at fenders and talking about great wrecks they had been in and how somebody ought to put up better signs and lights to prevent this sort of thing and how the wreck they had been in continued to play itself over and over in their mind months later.

The girl asked the forehead man to call someone where she worked. He walked over to a nearby office building and asked to use the phone, learning in the process that the police needed to be called again so they'd know the wreck included casualties. He walked back to the trapped woman and talked to her again, knowing she'd probably not remember anything said, but hoping the softness of the words would help till other help arrived.

An ambulance finally pulled up, just ahead of a city

emergency unit. The women in the ambulance were smiling and chatting. "Looks like everybody was called," they said, noting the city unit. They finally looked toward the car with the trapped woman and strolled over to look at her. A city policewoman was on the scene by now, making careful notes about the position of the cars, interviewing the standing driver and not noticing the young woman.

When at last the ambulance drivers began taking out equipment and actually dealing with the condition of the young woman, he finally drove away from the crowd and toward the bookshop, wondering whether the two people whose cars had collided, in the re-telling of their radically altered morning adventure, would act as casual as the limp but curious crowd, the bored officers and the sociably relaxed ambulance drivers had acted. And whether he himself had been anything more than a prurient viewer of just another random but very human event in a day like so many other days on whatever planet this is

—Jim Reed

DID THE EARTH MOVE FOR YOU?

A LITTLE AFTER SEVEN O'CLOCK ON SUNDAY MORNING.

The phone rings.

I flap my hand around to turn off the clock radio, which only begins to buzz loudly.

My hand then grabs the receiver of the phone and I mumble into it, nearly falling off the bed in the process.

It's Liz.

"Hello there!" I wonder whether something's wrong. After all, she's in Los Angeles and it should be a little after five o'clock on Sunday morning for her. She starts to speak but the buzzing clock drowns her out. I slap the radio a couple of times and lean down finally to pull the plug. Now I can hear.

"We've just had an earthquake," she says brightly. I'm wide awake now. Her voice is higher-pitched than usual, and she sounds cheerful. Or maybe it's the adrenalin. Her bed had vibrated for what seemed to be a full minute. She had called the hotel desk to see if there were some sort of procedure to follow in case of what seemed to be an earthquake. The desk clerk had said there was nothing to do about the situation, since the shaking seemed to have stopped.

"So, the earth moved for you this morning," I say, trying to sound as cheerful as she.

"My first earthquake," she remarks. We chat a bit and vow to talk again in a little while. I make my way downstairs to see what the media have to say about California this morning. As expected, our local crack news teams are nowhere to be found on the telly. Channel forty-two is running Andy Griffith, and Barney is going through some sort of identity crisis, as they used to say in the '70s. Channels six and thirteen, which run promotions 'round the clock boasting of mine's-bigger-than-yours news departments and sports teams and weather wizards, are blithely playing syndicated homogenized stuff, and so I turn to CNN to see what the only worldwide news network is doing.

Finally, a bit of news—just enough to let me know I

should keep worrying.

I call Liz back after the second earthquake, and we talk each other through the situation as much as possible when you're separated by thousands of miles and a handful of failing airlines. Then, we lose touch for a few hours, the airlines delay flights all over the place, connections are missed, and there's this Alabama wife in L.A. trying to get the hell out of Dodge so that she can return to the comfort of earthquake-free Alabama.

Once here, she can resume worrying about being in the tornado alley of the South—but then, tornadoes we're used to.

Earthquakes were invented by Californians to remind us of how much they like to live on the edge out there. Tornados are created wherever clusters of mobile homes appear. And everything in between tornados and earthquakes is the rest of the nation.

Who cares about all this? Right now, I just want my Liz back. What I dread most, though, is the prospect of having to go to bed tonight and try to re-program that damned clock radio

—*Jim Reed*

SPITZ JUNIOR

WHEN I WAS A YOUNG ONE just trying to absorb the fact that I'd never be a Babe Ruth or an Albert Einstein or an Edgar Allan Poe or a Gregory Peck, I received for Christmas (sitting there just beyond reach of the carnival-decorated, gaudy fir tree) a Spitz Junior Planetarium, manufactured by the "Harmonic Reed Corporation Of Rosemont, Penna."

It was a most special Christmas gift.

Just looking at it now, in my mind's eye, it has remained crystal-clear all these years: a shiny, black, flexible plastic globe bifurcated by a yellow rubber equatorial flange that represents the stellar ecliptic and incidentally holds the two half-spheres together. The black globe sits atop a white plastic observatory-shaped base, and the whole thing can be rotated round and round as well as moved up and down to simulate all the naked-eye observable movements of the stars.

To appreciate the planetarium, you had to take it into a pitch dark, preferably cube-shaped room and slowly turn up the rheostat just above the "off/on" switch on the front of the base. If you did it just right and just slowly enough, you would suddenly feel yourself transported to the middle of a darkened field in the middle of the night in the middle of the planet in the middle of the universe because, all around you, there would suddenly appear stars in exactly the same positions, the same configurations, as they would appear if you actually were in the middle of a darkened field in the middle of the night in the middle of . . . .

Even if you couldn't go outside to see the stars, even if it was cloudy and raining, even if you had just come indoors from the humid sunshine, you could still go into that darkened room and be somewhere else in time and space and feel all alone in a crowd of billions of others whose names you did not know.

Just a while ago, my sister Rosi got my Spitz Junior Planetarium out of storage and presented it to me and I took it home and now I sleep again in the middle of a darkened field in the middle of the night in the middle . . . .

Whenever the demon insomnia causes my eyes to flicker open, I can see the old familiar stars keeping me silent company and reminding me that they will always be there and that any problems that seem gargantuan now are minuscule compared to the distant silent coolness and the close-up noisy fury of those suns upon suns upon suns out there. The mathematics and physics of astronomy escaped me early on, but the sheer personal poetry of the tiny points of light so large and so far away still affect me and still make me remember what it was like to be a small boy and open an incredible shiny gift that pure and lonely Christmas so many eons ago in Tuscaloosa, Alabama

—*Jim Reed*

MERELY MUSING

IT SNUCK UP ON ME, like a padded-paw cat making so much noise a cobweb shuddered but nothing else.

It materialized just behind me and hovered there, its act of non-breathing disturbing only the little microbes that depend on living things' exhalations, but nothing else.

Whatever it was, it remained behind me no matter how hard I strained my neck trying to see, and it remained anonymous and invisible and invincible to any attempts to define it and find it and capture it and examine it.

It was there observing me or not observing me, I didn't know which. It smiled or did not smile and wouldn't let me know which. It either preferred me or knew nothing of my existence, and I couldn't tell anything at all about it except that it was there and it was present and it was as difficult to handwrestle as a butterfly's cough.

After a while I began to relax in its presence and even tried to ignore it, but I couldn't fool it and it couldn't fool me. No fooling.

I had to write about it, but I spent years trying not to, trying not to let on that I even knew it was there. Couldn't describe it to people, you know, because they'd think I was as weird as I am.

I even learned to talk to it, but like an orbiting Cheshire cat, it simply was amused or bemused or totally indifferent, but it stayed there, and I knew it had no importance except the importance that I would confer upon it.

So, finally, after running this way and that way and cringing and hiding and distracting myself with all manner of material devices, I decided it was about time "It" and I learned to co-exist. "It" did its thing (observing or not observing all that I did) and I did my thing (writing in its direction, composing and communicating who I was and was not on paper, writing and writing, no longer worrying that I would run dry). More guck and fun pressed down within than I could possibly write in a lifetime.

I learned from "It" that I can write because there's writing inside me that must be read. You can write, too—just as soon as you completely forget that other people claim they can write better, that their stuff is more important than yours, that their words are spelled better'n yours. Forget them, and pay attention to what's hovering behind you. Then, learn to ignore "It" and "Them" and get on with it. "It's" always there, but then so are you—and you can get those words out and down on paper just like the hundreds of thousands of writers before you who've populated the world with millions and millions of books and magazines and theses and documents and diaries and poems on napkins. And you, like all other writers, must remember that what you are writing is the most important thing in the world and, even if it's not read now or next generation, if you leave it where it's protected, it will indeed be read with wonder and delight someday by some person whom fate has decreed your reader. Your "It"

—Jim Reed

Winging It

WAR AND RUMORS OF WAR AND FAMINE AND FAST and furious competition among egocentric worldmongers aside, there are gentler things going on, too—no matter what you see on CNN or read in the doomsaying newsmags or see on the tiny silver screens located in concrete bunkers that are still euphemistically called "theatres."

Oh, to see a nice, sweet, thoughtful, and thoroughly interesting movie, to escape for a mere 120 minutes from all the stimulation and simulation of life that are hyped about us daily!

So . . . you can hear a movie recommendation coming, can't you? Alas, this one can only be obtained on videotape, since no profit-thinking theatre manager would show it for more than twenty-four hours (if that).

DAD'S TWEED COAT

Ready? Try to find a video store with integrity, dig diligently through the kung-phooey movies, the slash-and-bash R-rateds, the screeching tire and screaming bimbo flicks, and see if you can come up with *Wings of Desire*. No kidding. It's a nice and sweetly special film with—gasp—integrity. Don't let that scare you. It'll engross without grossing out, it'll entertain without bombast, it'll even make you think—and not only that, it'll make you think that being made to think isn't so bad once in a while. And it'll let you see that words, written words, can be translated to the screen with entertainment value—it just takes a little extra work and imagination on the part of the producers and directors.

Go ahead—don't be scared. I'll even let you in on the fact that one of the stars of this little German-French film is Peter Falk. It's even subtitled—but don't be put off by that, either. The subtitles are easy to read and well worth reading. I'm going to see this one again, and soon. Warning: You may wish to watch this film alone the first time—it's easy for the over-stimulated and cynical average video viewer to laugh at something so delicate

—*Jim Reed*

ALL THAT JESUS

OUTSIDE THE LARGE OLD WINDOWS OF THE CHURCH the bright Southside sunshine tried hard to get through the glass and closer to the sweet sounds of jazz, sounds that gently stroked the ceiling the floor the pews the people and the sunbeams themselves with variations on a theme of love thy everything.

The pews got harder the longer we sat but the music got lovelier and the lazy afternoon wouldn't loosen its hold on us.

Behind us an infant snored peacefully against its mother's breast and in front of us a little girl was so caught up in the music that her body vibrated with every chord, playing among the sunbeams and the old dust and the almost visible music notes and she was inside the music just as surely as the baby was inside his dreams inside his mother's arms and we sat in this hard pew between this infant and this child and felt the music so intimately that it seemed to be pulling our bodies together into one organic joy, even though we sat still and polite and quiet.

Jazz variations on Jesus or God or whomever each listener could invent to look up to and to appreciate outside themselves.

And that baby and that little girl couldn't tell jazz from Jesus and you know it really didn't matter, their purity was so resounding in the Sunday afternoon dust

—Jim Reed

INVISIBLE BIRTHDAY

WELL, THERE WAS MY OCTOGENARIAN MOTHER IN HER FLOWER-CHILD SKIRT and my fifty-year-old-plus sister Barbara (ain't I generous, Sis?) with a flower where her lapel should be and my forty-year-old-plus sister Rosi ready to break her Jennie Craig diet for a few minutes and my ageless wife, Liz (occasional bursts of diplomacy such as this is one of the ways I survive a lifetime relationship), and youthful me (hey, I'm the writer . . . it's good to be the writer!).

We're missing brother Tim, who's up North doing an art show, and brother Ronny, who's in Houston scouting for old books.

And, of course, we're permanently missing our

father, Tom, who died in 1987 but remains here in memory always green and whose birthday this is.

So, even though we have a bit of fun talking and gossiping and eating entirely too much at your average cookie-cutter yuppie restaurant, we never quite come out and mention the reason we're all symbolically huddling together just inside the cave entrance, out of sight of the sabre-toothed tigers and just prior to rolling the stone before the opening to sleep our respective sleeps. We converse and signify and joke and throw our metaphors at the ceiling and just feel each others' presences and most importantly the presence of our father who never really left us. Happy birthday, Daddy

—Jim Reed

Temple Bells

Standing in a stranger's front yard in the bright sun on a Saturday morning surrounded by good ol' boys and poofed-hair ladies may not be my idea of how to spend an hour or two of increasingly precious spare time but you know how us book lovers are—we'll go anyplace anytime in any circumstances to see whether there's a nice old volume or two worth picking up.

So there I was in somebody's yard in a cluster of middle-aged-up guys who were sniffing and poking a Lincoln Town Car which was to be auctioned off along with household goods that had somehow gotten possessed and protected by the court system.

Small wisdoms and unsolicited observations were

being passed about like hot potatoes and you somehow had the idea that these guys were playing poker, what with their stoic expressions and hands-in-pockets attitudes . . . trying to look disinterested and reserved but watching everything out of the corners of their eyes.

A faint tinkling was in the background, overriding everything so persistently that it was all but unnoticed. Finally, you realized that the almost temple-bell-like noise was coming from the insides of pockets times two dozen—the pockets where fidgety fingers continuously rattled loose change and car keys and good-luck charms.

The noise would continue till after the auction.

The house on the property was filled with strangers who had never even known the former occupants, and here all these strangers were, walking around, prodding previously-loved belongings that no longer belonged to anyone, no longer belonged to the people who first purchased them with great excitement, with great expectation that life would be slightly changed for the better as a result of the purchase, that life would forever be different and special if this object were kept and fondled now and then.

People sat on chairs and left grass stains on carpets and exhaled their stale internal airs, invading the once personal and very private atmosphere that not so long ago thrived in this suburban villa.

Somebody's past was about to be sold to the highest bidders, piece by truncated piece, and for a moment I felt like an interloper, an invader, but really I was just a preserver, dedicated to finding just the right thing to rescue and adopt and offer a safe home to and I would certainly do my minuscule part to extend the lifeline of some item, though I could never afford to rescue all the books in all the estate sales throughout the planet and ain't it about the most frustrating thing you as a fellow bookie could ever imagine

—*Jim Reed*

FINAL JOYS

WHAT WILL BE
That final thing that I can call my own?

Will it be the memory of me held inside my daughter
    and
granddaughter as they grow old and mellow?
Will it be the last copy of my book that finally becomes a
discard from some library fifty years hence?

What will be
That final thing that I can call my own?

Will it be that rolled-up note I left to myself inside the
ceiling of my parents' house some forty-five years ago?

Small Wisdoms, Hidden Comforts, Unexpected Joys

Will it be the final disappearing vestige of sound waves
produced by my laughter when I was three years old?

What will be
That final thing that I can call my own?

Will it be my final flashing memory of counting meteors
    as I
lay on the roof under the stars of my childhood home?
Will it be the last image of your face held tentatively by
my hands as I stargazed in your eyes?

What will be
That final thing that I can call my own?

—*Jim Reed*

POW Wow

REUNIONS CAN BE BORING OR FRIGHTENING OR JUST PLAIN FUN, but the reunion I'm attending right this minute this warm Friday night is none of the above because it is a reunion of military policemen, German ex-prisoners of war, and townspeople in the small community of Aliceville, Alabama.

More than fifty years ago nearly 6,000 captured German soldiers had been marched, shipped, and train-railed all the way from North Africa to Alabama, USA, where they had been cleansed, housed, fed, and incarcerated till the end of World War II made them no longer enemies of the Americas.

Now, all these decades later, some of the German POWs have returned with their families to the scene of their time, noble old ex-soldiers who feel as strongly about their wartime experiences as American soldiers do about their own.

A few of the stateside soldiers who were in charge of the prisoners way back then are on hand to greet them, as are Aliceville residents who knew them during their forced stay.

What a reunion! A kind of polite and genial inter-change occurs each year between the locals, who once feared or even hated the prisoners, the soldiers, who certainly were trained to kill or take prisoners, and the prisoners themselves, who should have resented their being held by an enemy they had been indoctrinated to resist.

But strangely enough, most of that fear, hatred, and misplaced dogma seemed to have disappeared within days of the German prisoners' arrival on enemy ground in the early 1940s. Once the citizens saw those tow-headed, unarmed young men marching into town from the train station, they noted the amazing resemblance between the sons of the enemy and their own sons.

The absentee sons who might never return home were replaced by foreign-accented youth who would live in their town, work in their fields, and slowly become friends for life with some of their neighbors.

The small museum we are visiting tonight is filled

with mementos of the wartime prison camp: art produced by German soldiers, gifts handmade and presented to their captors, uniforms and letters and official documents of war and photographs of faces like yours and mine, not to mention that right now we are munching on handmade, uncatered snacks that local women have lovingly prepared for this odd assortment of people.

And I am reminded of the stories my father used to tell us kids about the German prisoners he knew personally during the war in another town not so very far away—my hometown of Tuscaloosa.

Aliceville is a minuscule place that nobody goes through unless they're on the way to someplace else, but suddenly, this close and mellow Friday night, Aliceville seems like the biggest small town in the world, a town that disproves all the warmongers and all the former cold-war propagandists and everybody who ever looked real hard for a reason to hate some other people they'd never even met.

If this wonderful communion can occur in a town like Aliceville, why can't it occur anywhere and everywhere else in the world this coming Friday night

—Jim Reed

SHELF SPACE

HERE, IN ANACHRONISM HEAVEN, are all the big and little writers combined, living together in boxes on shelves on the floor propped up under things teetering on the edges of things squirreled away within containers of other things . . . writers who would not have been caught dead or alive together are thus now forced to be companions in my dusty little haven.

You have to wonder about all those living writers who go to all those "writer's conferences" and talk with one another about all their works-in-progress that haven't yet been made into books or all those books that have yet to be filmed or recorded on tape, and you wonder why they go.

DAD'S TWEED COAT

Why would anyone go to a writer's conference?

What? To be told how to write?

You already know how to write, and you don't need any prissy writer's conclave chairperson telling you how to change the name of your protagonist to "fit the market" and you don't need anyone telling you how to re-construct a sentence so that the reader will be less likely to put the book down prematurely.

No, to be a writer, you just need to write.

Write anything you want to write as badly or as nicely as you please, and don't listen to anyone who wants to make you over or edit you against your very personal judgment.

I decided a few eons ago that I no longer needed anybody to tell me how to write. Going to a couple of meetings where poor, low-self-esteem people were told by successfully published authors how much better than non-published writers they were killed the desire in me to listen to anybody who is an "expert." Instead, I decided that I would write what I write and put it into a bottle and float it into the accidental cosmos and hope that it will be read someday by someone who might need to read a lost message in a bottle for sustenance or inspiration or salvation . . . and, if the bottle never makes it anywhere, if Voyager never makes it anywhere, what does it matter anyhow if I got what I needed out of putting those words on that paper in that bottle or if the scientists who found joy in navigating that satellite into another solar system were satisfied with that moment of joy?

If the messages are received, OK. If not, at least they were sent in love and deeply felt while being composed just like this here message

—Jim Reed

A Breed Gone Dry

My father was born Easter Sunday in the year 1909, just ahead of Halley's Comet. His father placed his new infant in an Easter basket and presented him to his other half-dozen children, showing them what the Easter Bunny had brought them.

When my father died, we placed him in another beautiful basket, sending him on a journey the way he came in.

Our father (and our mother's husband) had to be

provider, comforter, counselor, stand-in, sometimes absentee disciplinarian, loving supporter, and cheer-leader.

Our father did just fine. (Mother's husband did just fine.) And we are all a little awed at how well he did his job.

The term "father" sounds a bit formal, doesn't it? We called him Daddy. Even at my advanced age, I still call him Daddy.

I hope this makes you sense just how we all felt about our daddy. And I hope, too, that you can find a way to see in your daddy the fine things we saw in ours. Even through bad times, we always knew Daddy had spent his entire life supporting us emotionally. His only goal was to bring us up and give us support.

He had no hobbies, no particular side interests, no diversions. He spent all his time being our daddy and Mother's husband. Perhaps the last of a special breed.

Anyhow, I hope you take a second look at your daddy—or the memory of your daddy. I hope you take a second look at your daddy and see what he was really there for all along: to lift you just one step higher toward heaven . . . to make you one ounce lighter toward heaven.

My father was a carpenter, a profession he felt he could really be proud of, since another man he admired, who had lived nearly 2,000 years before, had also practiced this profession.

When I was young, my father came home from work one day and gave me a book he had found in an old warehouse he and his crew had been clearing out.

The book was *The Rubaiyat of Omar Khayyam*, a man who lived centuries ago.

Omar understood life and accepted the consequences of life and pretty much tried to teach us that life is simply another stage of being . . . that life is to be cherished and appreciated, but that the end of life is simply another stage to be accepted and appreciated, too. I think my father understood that.

Here's what Omar said:

> Oh, come with old Khayyam, and leave the wise to
> talk;
> One thing is certain, that Life flies;
> One thing is certain, and the Rest is Lies;

The Flower that once has blown for ever dies.

There was a Door to which I found no key;
There was a Veil past which I could not see;
Some little Talk awhile of Me and Thee there
seemed—
And then no more of Thee and Me.

The Moving Finger writes; and, having writ, moves
on:
Nor all thy Piety nor Wit shall lure it back to cancel
half a line,
Nor all thy Tears wash out a word of it.

Omar has one last request. He wants to be buried in a garden, for in so doing he would be surrounded by those who came before him—since everybody rises from the ground and returns to it eventually. And he asks everyone to remember him each time they pass his place of burial:

And when you, with shining Foot shall pass among
the Guests Star-
scatter'd on The Grass, and in your joyous Errand

DAD'S TWEED COAT

    reach the spot
  where I made one—turn down an empty glass.

He was saying, "Smile and remember me."

So, Daddy, we who knew you best will remember the best.

And those who did not know you have missed something very important, something that can be found, with a little patience, in their own daddy.

Look for it. It is well worth the search

—Jim Reed

JUST ENOUGH LIFE

THERE'S JUST ENOUGH LIFE LEFT IN ME to catch a few thousand more sunrises, to laugh at nothing in particular a whole lot, to make the furrows on my shiny head a quarter-inch deeper, to fondly remember a few friends and relatives who are so much more real in my mind than they ever were in person.

There's just enough life left in me to fondle a lot more books, to smell the tobacco fragrance that the volume I'm holding absorbed a century ago from a reader who will only be remembered for his brand of smoke, to find a beautiful butterfly pressed within the pages of an 1866 issue of *Scribner's Magazine,* to open another love letter squirreled away inside an Eden Southworth volume seventy-five years ago—a letter from a long-gone love (did they ever marry, did they ever matter).

There's just enough life left in me to discover that this moment and all the other moments to come, should they come, are all that matters. This moment and the moments past and present that this moment connects are the moments that mean whether I am still alive, still in love, still suspiring, still grumbling and grinning and hacking away at the jungle that constantly attempts to obscure the obvious beauty that surrounds me.

There's just enough life left in you to hold a moment of my life in your hands as you read this and perhaps sense that on some minuscule level I am connected to you and it all may or may not matter but isn't it a lovely thought anyhow

—Jim Reed

LOOPING

I SAT THERE IN FRONT OF A GROUP OF PEOPLE who like to be called writers, but I wondered why they would call themselves writers since just about everybody writes (why not call themselves breathers since just about everybody breathes or why not call themselves humans since many of the people I know call themselves humans).

Why be called a writer?

I sat there in front of these people, wondering if some of them were hoping I'd say something that would in some way change their lives for the better, wondering at the same time if some of them were prepared in advance to be bored, wondering if one or two of them were asking themselves, "What gives this guy the right to stand before us and dare to speak on the subject of writing? What could he possibly say that I don't already know?"

Also wondering if some of them would rather be someplace else right now, perhaps on another planet, at least having a good cup of coffee in a South Pacific island paradise.

What made these particular people come to this particular place at this particular time to hear the words of a person they've never met before and would probably never meet again? I shifted my bottom to get a little more comfortable, glanced around the room at the expectant faces. Then, I paused, stared briefly at the ceiling, and uttered these words

—Jim Reed

PURPLE AND PINK

JUST ALL TOO RECENTLY, MY MOTHER DIED.

You would have enjoyed knowing her.

She was, among many other delightful things, a fiddler.

A non-musical fiddler is someone who fiddles around, doing things that are very important to the fiddler but of almost no importance to anyone else.

After knowing Mother for fifty-five years, I've come to understand and appreciate fiddlers, and indeed I've become a fiddler myself.

When she was alone, Mother loved nothing better

than to fiddle around in the yard, talking to her flowers and plants, chatting merrily with any animals that happened to stray into her line of vision, and exchanging pleasantries with folks who caught her eye.

She would trim, dig, plant, rearrange, fondle, dust, and wash anything at all that she came in contact with in her yard.

On days when she couldn't get outside, Mother would fiddle around inside the house, doing much the same things that she did outside, except that when house-bound, she would write notes and letters and cards. Much of the time these notes and letters and cards, jotted down on any scrap or pad that presented a paper surface, would be addressed to herself—notes about things she needed to do, notes about her feelings of happiness or anger and frustration, notes about things she hoped other people would do, notes about her hopes, notes about her small despairs.

Other notes would be left around the house and inside just about anything, and they would be notes about what she would like to do in the future, or notes that she hoped her family would read someday, or notes describing things she did not want our family to forget.

She left notes on the backs of hanging pictures and photographs, so that we would not forget who and what they were all about, and she never abandoned her firm belief that each and every note, each and every scrap of paper, was just as precious as all the wonderful stuff she accumulated over an eighty-three-year period.

Mother never willingly threw anything away, much to the joy of some of her children, much to the horror of some of her children.

Mother's home was a time capsule, and she always hoped that somebody would come along and appreciate each and every bit of paper and odds and ends as much as she had appreciated them.

So, not too long ago, we five brothers and sisters gathered at our childhood home and began unsealing Mother's time capsule. We spent our brief hours enjoying and reminiscing and mourning and remembering the one and only greatest fiddler of all time.

Soon after Mother's funeral, I dragged myself out the front door of our house in the middle of winter and made my way halfway down the sidewalk before I realized that for no reason at all our lone Japanese magnolia tree had pink-and-white-and-purple-blossomed itself into full beauty.

A fiddling tree that seemed infused with the sweetness of Mother's soul.

Purple and pink were Mother's favorite colors, you know.

Thanks for another note, Ma

—*Jim Reed*